Snap books®

Foolproof Frozen Treats

WITH A SIDE OF SCIENCE

An Augmented Recipe Science Experience

by M. M. Eboch

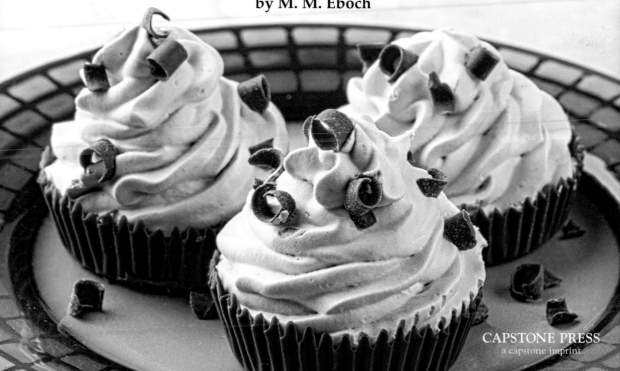

CAPSTONE PRESS
a capstone imprint

Download the Capstone app!

- Ask an adult to download the Capstone 4D app.

- Scan the cover and stars inside the book for additional content.

When you scan a spread, you'll find fun extra stuff to go with this book! You can also find these things on the web at www.capstone4D.com using the password: frozen.10706

Snap Books are published by Capstone Press, 1710 Roe Crest Drive,
North Mankato, Minnesota 56003
www.mycapstone.com

Library of Congress Cataloging-in-Publication Data
Names: Eboch, M. M., author.
Title: Foolproof frozen treats with a side of science : 4D an augmented
    recipe science experience / by M.M. Eboch.
Description: North Mankato, Minnesota : Capstone Press, 2019. | Series: Snap
    books. Sweet eats with a side of science 4D
Identifiers: LCCN 2018011853 (print) | LCCN 2018012778 (ebook) |
    ISBN 9781543510744 (eBook PDF) |
    ISBN 9781543510706 (library binding)
Subjects: LCSH: Frozen desserts—Juvenile literature. | LCGFT: Cookbooks.
Classification: LCC TX795 (ebook) | LCC TX795 .E26 2019 (print) | DDC
    641.86/2—dc23
LC record available at https://lccn.loc.gov/2018011853

Editorial Credits
Abby Colich, editor; Juliette Peters, designer; Tracy Cummins, media researcher;
Laura Manthe, production specialist

Photo Credits
Photo and Food Stylist: Sarah Schuette; All images by Capstone Studio/Karon Dubke,
except: Shutterstock: Ahanov Michael, 30 Bottom Right, AlenaKogotkova 30 Top Right, ffolas
30 Middle Right

Printed in the United States of America.
PA017

Table of Contents

Are you Ready to Chill?

Why do so many treats taste great cold? Juice, fruit, chocolate—you can freeze all sorts of things with surprisingly sweet success. You'll find many flavors among these frozen delights. Make a refreshing drink, a quick snack, or a delightful dessert. Some are as simple as a bowl of homemade ice cream or an ice pop on a stick. Others are so fancy you'll want to show them off to guests.

Making frozen treats is fun. If you follow the steps, your creation should turn out great. But understanding the science behind them will help make them foolproof. How do fat and sugar affect freezing? Why must ice cream be churned as it freezes? Do you really need to freeze the bowl before whipping cream? The answers are all part of the fascinating science that happens when you make frozen desserts!

SAFETY IS COOL ★

Hanging out in the kitchen and learning about science is fun as long as no one gets hurt. Make sure an adult is nearby to help, and follow these tips:

- Wash your hands well before you start. Wash them often while you work, especially after handling raw eggs.

- Avoid tasting uncooked mixtures if they contain eggs. Raw eggs may make you sick.

- Make sure an adult helps you anytime you need to use a sharp knife or food processor.

- Use pot holders or oven mitts to handle hot items. Don't touch any part of the inside of a hot oven.

- Clean up any spills.

NOW HEAD TO YOUR KITCHEN SCIENCE LAB FOR SOME TASTY EXPERIMENTS!

If you come across a cooking term or technique that you're not sure about, flip to page 30. Here you'll find more information about methods for mixing, boiling, and more!

CONVERSION CHART

The recipes in this book use U.S. measurements. If you need metric measurements, here's a handy conversion guide.

VOLUME

1/4 teaspoon = 1.2 mL
1/2 teaspoon = 2.5 mL
1 teaspoon = 5 mL
1 tablespoon = 15 mL
1/4 cup = 60 mL
1/3 cup = 80 mL
1/2 cup = 120 mL
2/3 cup = 160 mL
3/4 cup = 180 mL
1 cup = 240 mL

WEIGHT

1 ounce = 28 grams
3 ounces = 85 grams
3/4 pound = 340 grams

TIP

Many of these recipes require several hours to prepare and freeze. Allow enough time if you are planning to serve your dessert at a special event. You may want to prepare it the day before.

Frozen Lemonade Pops with Berry Skewers

Lemonade is tangy and sweet. It's the perfect drink for a hot day. What could be better than that? Lemonade ice pops! Yogurt makes these cool treats creamy. Rainbow sprinkles add fun colors. Skewered berries provide a tasty surprise. But you don't have to wait for a heat wave. Try this treat anytime!

INGREDIENTS

1/2 cup fresh raspberries
1/2 cup fresh blackberries
2 cups plain full-fat yogurt
2 tablespoons milk or nondairy milk
1/4 cup lemon juice
2 tablespoons honey
1/4 cup rainbow sprinkles

SUPPLIES

6 ice pop sticks
blender, optional
6 large ice pop molds or
    medium plastic or
    wax-coated cups,
    7 to 9 ounces

1 Skewer two to four berries on each ice pop stick. Push the stick through the middle of the berry. Alternate raspberries and blackberries. Set aside.

2 Mix the yogurt, milk, lemon juice, and honey in a blender or by hand. Blend until smooth. Taste a bit and add more lemon juice or honey if you wish.

3 Gently stir in the rainbow sprinkles. Pour the mixture into the ice pop molds or cups, filling each about halfway.

4 Gently insert the skewered ice pop sticks into the molds or cups. Top off the pops with more of the yogurt mixture. The pops will expand slightly as they freeze, so do not overfill.

5 Freeze until hard, at least 6 hours. To remove the pops from their molds, run them under warm water for 10 to 15 seconds.

Kitchen Science

FREEZING OR MELTING? ★

Every liquid has a temperature at which it typically turns into a solid. This is known as a freezing point. Plain water freezes at 32 degrees Fahrenheit (°F) or 0 degrees Celsius (°C). The freezing point for a liquid is usually the same as the melting point for the solid version of the same substance. In other words, ice (a solid) has a melting point of 32°F, when it becomes water. Water (a liquid) has a freezing point of 32°F, when it becomes ice. Other substances have different freezing points. Milk freezes at slightly below 32°F. Yogurt freezes at an even lower temperature.

Soda Shop Malted Ice Cream

Take a trip back in time to the days of ice cream parlors and malt shops. Malted milk powder gives chocolate ice cream a toasted caramel flavor. Malt powder contains several ingredients, but the grain barley gives it its flavor. Taste this ice cream and you'll understand why it's such a classic!

TIP.....................

Try your homemade ice cream in a milkshake! Blend 1 cup of the softened ice cream with 1/4 cup milk for each shake.

INGREDIENTS	SUPPLIES
3 ounces unsweetened chocolate	knife or food processor
2/3 cup sugar	medium saucepan
1/2 cup malted milk powder	whisk
1/4 cup cocoa powder	medium bowl
2 cups whole milk	measuring cups and spoons
1/2 cup heavy whipping cream	large storage container
2 eggs	ice cream maker, or chilled cake pan
1 tablespoon vanilla extract	and electric mixer or blender
1/4 teaspoon salt	
whipped cream and cherries, optional	

1 Finely chop the unsweetened chocolate with a knife or in a food processor.

2 In a saucepan, blend the sugar, malted milk powder, cocoa powder, and chopped chocolate. Whisk in the milk and cream. Cook over medium heat, stirring often, until the mixture is smooth and combined. Remove from heat.

3 Break the eggs into a medium bowl and whisk them. Very slowly pour one cup of the hot mixture into the eggs, whisking continuously. Make sure it is well blended. Then slowly pour the egg mixture back into the saucepan with the rest of the milk mixture. Be sure to add the mixture slowly so the eggs do not cook into strands. Stir continuously as you combine them.

4 Cook on very low heat, stirring constantly, for about 2 minutes. The mixture should thicken enough to leave a coating on the back of a spoon.

5 Remove the saucepan from the heat. Whisk in the vanilla extract and salt.

6 Pour the mixture into a storage container and seal it. Refrigerate at least 2 hours, up to overnight.

7 Pour the mixture into the canister of an ice cream maker. Freeze according to manufacturer's instructions. If you don't have an ice cream maker, pour the mixture into a cake pan that's been chilled in the freezer. Freeze for 45 minutes. Take out and blend with an electric mixer or blender. Return to the freezer and repeat every 30 minutes for 2 to 3 hours until frozen.

8 Serve in a bowl and top with whipped cream and cherries if you'd like.

Kitchen Science

WATER VERSUS ICE

Water is made up of molecules. These are the smallest part of a substance. They are too small to see without a microscope. As a liquid, water molecules move around each other. But when water freezes into ice, the water molecules arrange into structures called ice crystals. The lower the temperature, the more quickly water freezes. The ice crystals stay small. When temperatures are closer to freezing (32°F or 0°C), water turns to ice more slowly. The ice crystals are larger. Large ice crystals can affect a food's texture, making it grainy. An ice cream maker prevents large ice crystals from forming by churning, or mixing, the liquid ingredients as they freeze. That's also why you need to take the ice cream out of the freezer and stir if you're not using an ice cream maker. Stirring helps keep large ice crystals from forming.

Root Beer Granita Parfait

Granita is a frozen dessert made from water, sugar, and other ingredients. It has a flaky, icy texture. It's like eating snow! This root-beer-flavored granita is topped with homemade vanilla ice cream for a delicious, refreshing combo.

INGREDIENTS

1 1/2 cups heavy whipping cream
1 1/2 cups half and half
2/3 cup white sugar
2 teaspoons vanilla extract
6 cups root beer

SUPPLIES

large bowl
measuring cups and spoons
whisk
plastic wrap
baking dish,
　　at least 9 x 9 inches (23 x 23 cm)
ice cream maker, or chilled cake pan
　　and electric mixer or blender
glass mugs or parfait glasses

1 Start the vanilla ice cream first. In a large bowl, stir together the heavy whipping cream and half-and-half. Slowly pour in the sugar and whisk until blended. Whisk in the vanilla extract. Cover with plastic wrap. Refrigerate for at least 3 hours up to overnight.

2 Meanwhile, start the root beer granita. Pour the root beer into the baking dish. Cover tightly with plastic wrap. Clear space in the freezer so you can lay the dish flat. Freeze for 45 minutes.

3 Remove the root beer from the freezer. Stir briskly, mixing together the frozen and less frozen portions. Return it to the freezer until frozen solid, at least 3 hours up to overnight.

4 Place the ice cream mixture in the canister of an ice cream maker. Freeze according to the manufacturer's directions. If you don't have an ice cream maker, pour the mixture into a cake pan that's been chilled in the freezer. Freeze for 45 minutes. Take out and blend with an electric mixer or blender. Return to the freezer and repeat every 30 minutes for 2 to 3 hours until frozen.

5 Remove the frozen root beer from the freezer. Use a fork to scrape the granita into icy flakes. Return it to the freezer for at least 1 hour, or until the ice cream is ready.

6 When the ice cream is finished, transfer it to the freezer until you are ready to serve.

7 To serve, alternate layers of granita and vanilla ice cream in the parfait glasses or goblets. Serve immediately.

Kitchen Science

EXPLOSIONS IN THE FREEZER! ★

As water freezes and forms into ice crystals, it expands. Ice takes up about 10 percent more space than liquid water. This is why you should never leave a sealed soda can or water bottle in the freezer. When it freezes, it expands and may explode! In this recipe, pouring the root beer into a larger container gives it room to expand. The root beer granita has a flakier texture because ice crystals are allowed to form as it freezes. Stirring ice cream as it freezes or using an ice cream maker keeps its texture smooth.

So Peachy Frozen Yogurt

Juicy, ripe peaches are a summer treat that can't be beat—unless they're turned into a frozen dessert! Fresh peaches and vanilla make a rich, homemade frozen yogurt. Top the dish with more peaches sautéed in butter and a touch of cinnamon and honey. It's peachy perfection!

INGREDIENTS	TOPPING	SUPPLIES
2 ripe peaches 4 cups full-fat yogurt 1/2 cup half and half 2/3 cup honey 2 teaspoons vanilla extract	4 peaches 2 tablespoons butter 1 tablespoon honey 1/4 teaspoon cinnamon	sharp knife blender measuring cups and spoons ice cream maker, or chilled cake pan and electric mixer saucepan slotted spoon large sauté pan or skillet

1 Wash and cut the peaches into 1-inch (2.5-cm) chunks. Discard the pits. In a blender, mix the diced peaches, yogurt, half-and-half, honey, and vanilla extract. Blend until smooth.

2 Pour the mixture into an ice cream maker and freeze according to the manufacturer's instructions. If you don't have an ice cream maker, pour the mixture into a cake pan that's been chilled in the freezer. Freeze for 45 minutes. Take out and blend with an electric mixer or blender. Return to the freezer and repeat every 30 minutes for at least 3 hours until frozen. The result will be the consistency of soft serve ice cream. If you want it harder, pour the mixture into another container. Freeze it an additional 2 hours or more.

3 For the topping, peel the remaining peaches. To do this, place them in a saucepan of boiling water for 10 to 20 seconds. Remove them with a slotted spoon and drop them into very cold water for 30 to 60 seconds. The skin should slip off easily. If it doesn't, ask an adult to help you use a paring knife to finish the job. Slice the peaches into wedges.

4 Melt the butter over medium heat in a sauté pan or skillet. Add the sliced peaches. Sauté for 3 minutes.

5 Add the honey and cinnamon. Sauté for an additional minute. Remove from the heat and let cool.

6 Serve the peach frozen yogurt with the sautéed peaches on top. The sautéed peaches can be added warm, at room temperature, or after being chilled in the fridge.

TIP ·

If fresh peaches are not available, use frozen or canned sliced peaches. You'll need about 1 cup to replace each fresh peach.

Kitchen Science

FREEZING FATS

Ice cream is creamy because it contains fat from cream. When fat freezes, it stays in blobs or only partly crystallizes. This keeps it from turning grainy. Yogurt may seem creamy, but it actually has a lot of water in it. When this water freezes, it forms crystals, which have a grainy texture. That means simply freezing yogurt may turn it into a grainy, unpleasant mess. This is especially true if you use low-fat or nonfat yogurt. When making frozen yogurt, start with full-fat yogurt. In this recipe, the half and half also adds creaminess and reduces the amount of water.

Rocky Road Pudding Pops

When you first hear the name rocky road, it might not sound like an appetizing ice cream flavor. Who would think of such a thing? Several people claimed they invented this ice cream flavor. Does it really matter who decided to add nuts and marshmallows to chocolate ice cream? Let's thank them and move on by making your own rocky road ice pops.

INGREDIENTS

1/2 cup sugar
2 tablespoons corn starch
1/4 teaspoon salt
1 egg
2 cups milk
1 cup chocolate chips
1 ounce unsweetened chocolate

2 tablespoons butter
2 teaspoons vanilla extract
1/2 cup chopped peanuts
1/2 cup miniature
   chocolate chips
1 cup miniature marshmallows

SUPPLIES

measuring cups and spoons
medium nonstick pot
heatproof rubber spatula
12 3-ounce disposable waxed
   paper or plastic cups
12 ice pop sticks

1 Mix sugar, corn starch, and salt in a nonstick pot. Add the egg and milk and blend well. Add chocolate chips and unsweetened chocolate.

2 Place the pot on the stove at medium-high heat. Stir continuously, scraping the bottom with a heatproof rubber spatula. Cook until gently bubbling, thick and smooth, about 5 to 10 minutes.

3 Remove from heat. Stir in the butter and vanilla extract. Let cool for at least 30 minutes.

4 Combine peanuts and miniature chocolate chips. Spoon about 2 tablespoons of the mixture into each of the cups.

5 Blend miniature marshmallows into the cooled pudding. Divide this mixture among the cups.

6 Add some of the remaining nut and chip mixture to the top of each cup. Insert an ice pop stick into each cup. Freeze until solid, at least 1 hour.

Apple and Honey Sorbet

Frozen applesauce? Why not! Sorbet is a frozen dessert made from fruit juice or flavored water. This apple sorbet may seem plain and simple, but take a closer look—and taste. This recipe uses whole apples instead of juice for a bolder flavor. It's tangy, tart, and sweet. Apple skins give the sorbet some red and green flecks of color.

INGREDIENTS

3/4 pounds (340 g) tart green apples,
    such as Granny Smith
3/4 pounds (340 g) tart red apples,
    such as Cameo, Jonagold, or Baldwin
3 tablespoons lemon juice
1 1/2 cups water
1 cup sugar
1/4 cup honey
1/4 teaspoon cinnamon
mint sprigs for garnish

SUPPLIES

sharp knife
large plastic container with lid
measuring cups and spoons
small saucepan
blender
ice cream maker or chilled cake pan

1 Core all the apples. Discard the cores. Slice the apples very thinly.

2 Put the apple slices and lemon juice in the plastic container. Seal the lid and shake to combine. Freeze at least 3 hours, up to overnight.

3 In a small saucepan, combine water and sugar. Bring to a boil, reduce heat, and simmer for 5 minutes.

4 Remove saucepan from the heat. Stir in the honey and cinnamon. Let cool completely, for at least 1 hour.

5 Place the apples, lemon juice, and sugar syrup in a blender. Blend until very smooth. You'll be able to see the small flecks of peel.

6 Transfer the mixture to an ice cream maker. Freeze according to the manufacturer's directions. If you don't have an ice cream maker, pour the blended mixture onto a chilled cookie sheet. Freeze until firm. Break it into chunks and return them to the blender. Blend until smooth. Repeat one more time for a smoother sorbet.

7 Soften the sorbet for 10 minutes at room temperature before serving. Decorate each serving with a sprig of fresh mint.

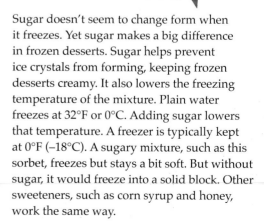

Kitchen Science

SWEET FREEZE ★

Sugar doesn't seem to change form when it freezes. Yet sugar makes a big difference in frozen desserts. Sugar helps prevent ice crystals from forming, keeping frozen desserts creamy. It also lowers the freezing temperature of the mixture. Plain water freezes at 32°F or 0°C. Adding sugar lowers that temperature. A freezer is typically kept at 0°F (–18°C). A sugary mixture, such as this sorbet, freezes but stays a bit soft. But without sugar, it would freeze into a solid block. Other sweeteners, such as corn syrup and honey, work the same way.

Chocolate Mousse in Chocolate Cups

Some dishes make food look pretty, but they're usually forgotten when the meal is over. But no one will forget bowls made out of chocolate! They're filled with fluffy, frozen chocolate mousse and decorated with chocolate shavings. This dessert will certainly impress your party guests.

INGREDIENTS

1 cup chocolate chips
1 tablespoon butter
1 cup sugar
1 cup baking cocoa
3 cups whipping cream
2 teaspoons vanilla extract
chocolate shavings to decorate

SUPPLIES

8 cupcake liners
muffin tin
nonstick cooking spray
microwave-safe bowl
pastry brush
mixing bowl
measuring cups and spoons
electric mixer

1 Place eight cupcake liners in the muffin tin. Spray them with nonstick cooking spray.

2 Place the chocolate chips and butter in a microwave-safe bowl. Heat at 50 percent power for 1 minute. Then stir. Heat for additional 30-second intervals as necessary, until the chocolate is smooth.

3 Divide the chocolate among the eight cupcake liners. Using a pastry brush, brush the chocolate evenly on the inside of each cupcake liner.

4 Chill the chocolate cups in the refrigerator until hardened, at least 30 minutes.

5 In a mixing bowl, combine the sugar and cocoa. Blend in the whipping cream and vanilla extract. Beat with an electric mixer until the mixture forms into soft peaks.

6 Remove the chocolate cups from the refrigerator. Check for any holes. Patch them with a dollop of melted chocolate. Peel off the liners and discard them. Put the bowls back into the cupcake pan. Divide the chocolate mousse among the chocolate cups. Freeze for at least 2 hours.

7 Decorate the chocolate mousse with chocolate shavings. Serve immediately.

TIP ....

This recipe asks you to mix until soft peaks form. To test your peaks, stop the mixer and lift the beater. The mix is ready when the beater leaves a peak or point in the mixture, and the top of the peak curls down.

Three-Toned Fruity Smoothie

What frozen snack is as delicious as it is healthy? The fruit smoothie, of course! The fruit packs nutritional goodness into each glass. With three layers of color and fun toppings, these smoothies look as pretty as they taste.

INGREDIENTS	SUPPLIES
1 cup blueberry yogurt	sharp knife
1 cup frozen blueberries	blender
1 cup milk or nondairy milk, separated	measuring cups
1 cup strawberry yogurt	6 tall glasses
1 cup frozen strawberries	
1 large, ripe banana	
1 cup vanilla yogurt	
1/2 cup fresh blueberries	
6 fresh strawberries	
whipped cream, optional	

1 Place the blueberry yogurt, frozen blueberries, and 1/4 cup milk in the blender. Blend smooth. If necessary, add more milk for consistency. Divide the mixture among the glasses, filling each no more than one-third full.

2 Clean and dry the blender. Place the strawberry yogurt, frozen strawberries, and 1/4 cup milk in the blender. Blend smooth. If necessary, add more milk for consistency. Divide this among the glasses, on top of the blueberry mixture. The glasses should now be about two-thirds full.

3 Clean and dry the blender. Cut the banana into 1-inch (2.5-cm) pieces. Place the banana, vanilla yogurt, and 1/2 cup milk in the blender. Blend until smooth. Check the consistency. You want to be able to drink it through a straw. If necessary, add up to another 1/4 cup milk. Divide this among the glasses, on top of the other two colors.

4 To garnish, sprinkle with fresh blueberries. Top with a fresh strawberry and add a bit of whipped cream if you'd like.

TIP . . . .

If a recipe says that an ingredient is separated, it means that the whole ingredient will not be used at once. Read through the recipe to see how much is needed at one time.

Hot Chocolate Pops Surprise

Frozen hot chocolate? That's right. You can enjoy the rich, cozy flavor of hot chocolate even on a hot day! Inside the frozen cocoa is a chewy marshmallow coated in caramel. You won't want to go back to plain old hot chocolate in a mug ever again!

INGREDIENTS	FILLING INGREDIENTS	SUPPLIES
1/2 cup unsweetened cocoa powder 1/4 cup sugar 1/4 teaspoon salt 4 cups milk or nondairy milk 1 teaspoon vanilla extract	1 packed cup brown sugar 1/2 cup half and half 1/4 cup butter pinch of salt 2 teaspoons vanilla extract 6 regular marshmallows	2 medium saucepans measuring cups and spoons 6 medium ice pop molds, or plastic or wax-coated cups, 7 to 9 ounces 6 ice pop sticks

1 Make the hot cocoa first. Combine the cocoa powder, sugar, and salt in a saucepan. Stirring constantly, add just enough milk to make a paste. Turn the heat to medium-low. Slowly add the rest of the milk, stirring constantly. Cook until the mixture is hot and the cocoa and sugar are fully dissolved.

2 Remove the saucepan from the heat. Blend in the vanilla extract. Let the cocoa cool to room temperature.

3 Meanwhile, make the caramel sauce. In a clean saucepan, mix the brown sugar, half and half, butter, and salt. Heat at medium-low, stirring gently the whole time, until thickened, about 5 to 7 minutes. Let cool.

4 Insert one end of an ice pop stick into a marshmallow. Let the stick poke out about 0.5 inch (1 cm). Dip the marshmallow in caramel sauce, turning to get it fully coated. Place the stick, marshmallow side down, into a cup. Repeat to fill the remaining cups.

5 Pour the cooled cocoa into the molds or cups, filling around and over the marshmallow. Don't fill completely. Leave room for the mixture to expand as it freezes.

6 Freeze until solid, about 6 hours. Remove from molds to serve.

TIP..............................

If you use round or square ice pop molds for this recipe instead of cups, make sure they are big enough to fit the marshmallows.

Mini Key Lime Pies

If you like tart treats, this dessert is for you! The creamy, lime-infused filling is balanced by the sweet, buttery graham cracker crust. Candied lime slices add another touch of tartness plus a pretty design. You don't have to serve these on sticks, but it makes them more fun to eat!

INGREDIENTS

6 tablespoons butter
1 1/2 cups graham cracker
    crumbs
1/3 cup sugar
1 can (14 ounces) sweetened
    condensed milk
1 tablespoon grated lime peel
1/2 cup lime juice, preferably
    key lime
2 cups whipped topping

CANDIED LIME SLICES

2 large or 3 small limes
1 cup water
1 cup sugar, plus 1/4 cup

SUPPLIES

mixing bowls
measuring cups and spoons
muffin pan
8 cupcake liners
nonstick cooking spray
medium pot
sharp knife
slotted spoon
wire cooling rack
waxed paper or cookie sheet
sturdy ice pop sticks

1 Put the butter in a medium, microwave-safe bowl. Microwave for 30 seconds at a time, stirring until fully melted. Mix in the graham cracker crumbs and sugar.

2 Line the muffin pan with eight cupcake liners and spray them with nonstick cooking spray. Divide the crumb mixture among the cupcake liners. Spread it evenly over the bottom and sides, pressing down firmly.

3 In a large bowl, combine the sweetened condensed milk, grated lime peel, and lime juice. Blend well. Gently fold in the whipped topping.

4 Scoop the mixture into the graham cracker crusts and spread evenly. Freeze until firm, about 4 hours.

5 Meanwhile, make the candied lime slices. Slice the fresh limes into thin circles, about 1/8 inch (0.3 cm) thick. Remove any seeds.

6 In a medium pot, mix the water and 1 cup of the sugar. Bring to a simmer, stirring to dissolve the sugar. Add the lime slices and simmer, stirring occasionally. Cook until the white pith (the inner layer of the peel) looks clear, about 15 minutes.

7 Using a slotted spoon, remove the limes. Spread them on a cooling rack in a single layer. Let them dry for 1 hour up to overnight. Put a sheet of waxed paper or a cookie sheet under the cooling racks to catch drips from the limes.

8 Put the remaining 1/4 cup of sugar in a small bowl. Press the lime slices into the sugar, coating both sides.

9 Take a few sugared lime slices and gently press them onto the top of a pie in a pattern. Repeat for each pie. If the lime slices are too large for the top of one pie, cut them into triangles, like slices of pizzas.

10 Remove the cupcake liners from the pies. Slide an ice pop stick into the pie. If the pie is too frozen, let it thaw for a bit and try again. Place the pies on a baking sheet and freeze them for at least 1 hour longer.

TIP ....

If starting with full graham cracker squares, you'll need about 20 squares. Put them in a plastic baggie, seal it, and crush them with a rolling pin. You can also use a food processor to make crumbs.

Tropical Dream Sorbet Cake

Take your taste buds to a tropical paradise! Pineapple, mango, and banana will make you feel like you're someplace warm and tropical. Coconut milk adds another classic flavor from the tropics. Plus it makes this dessert dairy-free and vegan! The sorbets are stacked and sliced for a festive, fruity feast.

INGREDIENTS

1 1/2 cups sweetened, shredded coconut
2 cups sliced bananas
1/2 teaspoon vanilla extract
1 1/2 cups frozen pineapple chunks
1 can full-fat coconut milk
2 tablespoons maple syrup or honey, separated
1 1/2 cups frozen mango chunks

SUPPLIES

baking sheet
wire cooling rack
blender or food processor
freezer-safe containers
8.5- x 4.5-inch (22- x 11.5-cm) loaf pan
plastic wrap
cutting board
serrated knife

1 Preheat oven to 350°F. Spread the shredded coconut on a baking sheet. Bake for 2 to 3 minutes. Stir the coconut and re-spread it every 2 to 3 minutes, until it turns golden, about 8 to 10 minutes. Set the baking sheet on a wire rack. Let cool completely.

2 Place the sliced bananas and vanilla extract in a blender or food processor. Blend until smooth. Pour the mixture into a freezer container and freeze until needed.

3 Clean and dry the blender or food processor. Shake the can of coconut milk to mix it well before opening. Add half of the can, the pineapple chunks, and 1 tablespoon maple syrup or honey to the blender or food processor. Blend until smooth. Pour the pineapple sorbet into a freezer container and freeze until needed.

4 Clean and dry the blender or food processor. Add the remaining coconut milk, mango chunks, and 1 tablespoon maple syrup or honey. Blend until smooth. Pour the mango sorbet into a freezer container and freeze until needed.

5 Line the loaf pan with a long strip of plastic wrap. Leave several inches overhanging on the long sides. Sprinkle one-third of the toasted coconut evenly along the bottom of the loaf pan. Drop spoonfuls of banana sorbet on top and spread evenly.

6 Sprinkle half of the remaining shredded coconut on top of the banana sorbet. Drop spoonfuls of pineapple sorbet on top, and spread evenly.

7 Sprinkle the remaining shredded coconut on top of the pineapple sorbet. Drop spoonfuls of mango sorbet on top, and spread evenly.

8 Fold the overhanging plastic wrap over the sorbet. Freeze until firm, at least 6 hours. You can keep it in the freezer for up to 2 weeks.

9 To serve, unfold the plastic. Turn the loaf pan upside down onto a cutting board. Peel off the plastic. Slice the sorbet cake with a serrated knife. If the sorbet is too hard to spread, microwave it for 10 seconds at a time, testing for softness in between. Sprinkle with more toasted shredded coconut if desired.

TIP

If using fresh mangoes and pineapple, prepare the fruit ahead of time. Peel the fruits, slice them, and freeze them, each in a separate container. Freeze for several hours up to a day.

Elegant Chocolate Mint Pie

You'll hear oohs and ahhs over this delectable dessert! A baked meringue crust is filled with chocolate chip mint ice cream and topped with chocolate sauce. This takes some time to put together, but it's well worth the wait.

TIP . . . .

For stiff peaks, the mixture will hold firmly onto the bottom of the beater. For medium peaks, the mixture will hold, but the tips will fall over.

INGREDIENTS

3 egg whites
1/4 teaspoon cream of tartar
2 to 3 drops green
   food coloring
1 cup sugar

FILLING INGREDIENTS

1/4 cup butter
1 ounce unsweetened chocolate
1 cup sugar
3/4 cup evaporated milk
1/2 teaspoon vanilla extract
pinch of salt
1 1/2 cups heavy whipping cream
2 tablespoons confectioners' sugar
1/2 teaspoon peppermint extract
2 cups chocolate chip mint
   ice cream

SUPPLIES

9-inch (23-cm) deep-dish
   pie pan
butter and flour for greasing
   the pan
mixing bowls
electric mixer
measuring cups and spoons
heavy saucepan
metal mixing bowl

1 Preheat oven to 275°F. Grease and flour the pie pan. Separate egg whites from the yolks. Crack the eggs over a mixing bowl. Transfer the yolk between each half of the cracked egg, letting the whites fall into the bowl, until all the white has fallen. Save the yolks for another use or discard.

2 Beat the egg whites with an electric mixer until foamy. Add the cream of tartar and food coloring. Beat until soft peaks form. Pour in the sugar very slowly, beating continuously. Keep beating until stiff, glossy peaks form.

3 Gently spread the meringue onto the bottom and up the sides of the pie pan. Bake for 1 hour. Then turn off oven but do not open the oven door. Let the meringue cool completely inside the oven.

4 Clean and dry the beaters for the electric mixer. Place them and a metal mixing bowl into the freezer for at least 15 minutes.

5 Meanwhile, make the chocolate sauce. In a heavy saucepan, melt the butter and chocolate over medium-low heat. Stir until smooth. Blend in the sugar and evaporated milk. Cook over low heat for 45 to 60 minutes or until thickened, stirring occasionally. Remove from the heat and stir in the vanilla extract and salt. Cool to room temperature.

6 Combine the whipping cream, confectioners' sugar, and peppermint extract in the chilled metal bowl. Mix with the electric mixer for about 1 minute, until medium peaks form.

7 Gently fold the whipped cream into the cooled chocolate sauce.

8 Spread the ice cream into the meringue crust. If the ice cream is too hard to spread easily, microwave it for 10 seconds at a time, testing for softness in between.

9 Spread chocolate sauce over the ice cream layer. Freeze until firm.

Kitchen Science

KEEP IT COLD

Expert cooks know that cold whipping cream whips more easily than if it's warm. It also has a smoother texture. Why? Whipping blends air bubbles into the cream. These air bubbles are held in place by fat droplets in the cream. When the whipping cream is cold, the tiny drops of solid fat stay solid. When they are solid, they can hold the air bubbles in place better. The whipped cream is light and airy. If the cream is warmer, the fat droplets soften, collapse, and form small clumps. The cream won't be as fluffy, and the texture will be grainy. Leave cream in the refrigerator until you're ready to whip it. Chilling the bowl and beaters in the freezer before using them helps keep the cream cold too.

Cooking Help

You don't have to be a master chef to successfully make these frozen treats. Here are some kitchen basics for those who are new to dessert making or for those who need to brush up on their knowledge.

DON'T MIX UP THE MIXING

Some recipes ask you to mix ingredients by hand, while others may require you to use an electric mixer. To mix something by hand, simply stir together with a spoon until the ingredients are combined. The same goes for an electric mixer. If a recipe asks you to beat ingredients, start with the lowest speed and slowly increase as needed.

WHIP OUT THAT WHISK

What do you do if a recipe asks you to whisk ingredients? Quickly move the whisk from side to side. It helps bring air into the ingredients, making them foamy or fluffy. If you don't have a whisk, use two forks faced together.

KNOW YOUR FOLDS

Folding is a method of gently mixing ingredients. It's used when the mixture has a lot of air that you don't want to release. Use a rubber spatula. Run it along the side of the mixture, across the bottom of the bowl, and back up. This brings some of the mixture from the bottom up to the top.

ON THE STOVE

For recipes that require stove cooking, be sure you know the difference between boiling and simmering.

Boiling is when bubbles rise and break on the surface of the liquid.

In a simmer, tiny bubbles will break the surface once in a while.

Glossary

crystal—a solid material where the parts are arranged in a geometric form

crystallize—to form or organize into the shape of crystals

freezing point—the temperature at which a liquid turns into a solid

ice crystals—water molecules frozen into hard, microscopic shapes

melting point—the temperature at which a particular solid will melt

mixture—a combination of two or more substances that are mixed together but not chemically combined together

molecule—the smallest particle of a substance that retains all the properties of that substance

sauté—to cook in butter or oil

structure—an arrangement of parts

temperature—a measure of how hot or cold something is

Read More

Bader, Bonnie. *Curious About Ice Cream.* Smithsonian. New York: Penguin Young Readers, 2017.

Cobb, Vicki. *Science Experiments You Can Eat.* New York: HarperCollins, 2016.

Hammer, Melina. *Kid Chef: The Foodie Kids Cookbook: Healthy Recipes and Culinary Skills for the New Cook in the Kitchen.* Berkeley, Calif.: Sonoma Press, 2016.

Internet Sites

Use FactHound to find Internet sites related to this book.

Visit *www.facthound.com*

Just type in 9781543510706 and go.

 Check out projects, games and lots more at
www.capstonekids.com